INK
Rules of Success
No matter where you go, there you are.

The secret of success is sincerity.
Once you can fake that you've got it made

The Rules of Success

an A to Z of Lifelaws

revealed by Roger Kilroy

illuminated by Ed McLachlan

Futura
Macdonald & Co
London & Sydney

A Futura Book

First published in Great Britain by Futura,
a division of Macdonald & Co,
London & Sydney

ISBN: 0 7088 2199 5

Printed in Great Britain by
Richard Clay (The Chaucer Press) Ltd,
Bungay, Suffolk

Futura Publications
A division of Macdonald & Co (Publishers) Ltd
Maxwell House
Worship Street
London EC2A 2EN

CONTENTS

RULE FOR FOREWORD WRITERS

Keep 'em short — no one reads 'em

FOREWORD

There was a time when all natural laws and principles seemed to belong to either Archimedes, Einstein or Newton, but in an age when computer software has taken most of the fun out of scientific and human discovery, people have been applying their wetware to a new generation of laws of a rather different sort. Persuasive, pointed, pithy (and steeped in ageless oracular wisdom) these new Lifelaws and Official Rules cover every aspect of our lives, from love and marriage to death and indebtedness, from going to work to missing the bus. The best of these laws we've collected in the pages that follow and if you study them carefully they should help lead you to that most tantalising of goals: success in all that you do. What we are offering you is quite simply a unique A–Z of rules, laws and maxims guaranteed to make you healthy, wealthy and wise.*

* Sexy too.

Absolute
Laws

MURPHY'S LAW

If anything can go wrong, it will.

CHEOP'S LAW

Nothing ever gets built on schedule or within budget.

NIXON'S LAW

If two wrongs don't make a right — try three!

LAW OF DELAY

Simple jobs always get put off because there will be time to do them later.

LAW OF THE SEARCH
The first place to look for anything is the last place you would expect to find it.
LAW OF PERVERSITY OF NATURE
You cannot successfully determine beforehand which side of the bread to butter.
LAW OF THE EYE AND THE STOMACH
When eating an elephant, take one bite at a time.

LAW OF LIFE
1-Those who can—do.
2-Those who cannot—teach.
3-Those who cannot teach
-teach teachers to teach.
4-Those who cannot teach teachers
to teach—administrate.
1
2
3
4

ARMY LAW

If it moves, salute it ;
If it doesn't move pick it up;
If you can't pick it up, paint it.

Business as usual!

THE LAWS OF OFFICE LIFE

The one time in the day that you lean back and relax is the one time the boss walks through the office.

Teamwork is essential —

IF YOU HAVE A DIFFICULT TASK, GIVE IT TO A LAZY MAN — HE WILL FIND AN EASIER WAY TO DO IT.

The phone will not ring until you leave your desk and walk to the other end of the building.

It allows you to blame someone else.

THE SUMPTUOUSNESS OF A COMPANY'S ANNU
REPORT IS IN INVERSE PROPORTION TO IT
PROFITABILITY THAT YEAR.

TREATMENT OF CONSPICUOUS SUCCESS

In any organisation there will alway
be one person who knows what is going o
— THIS PERSON MUST BE FIRED!!

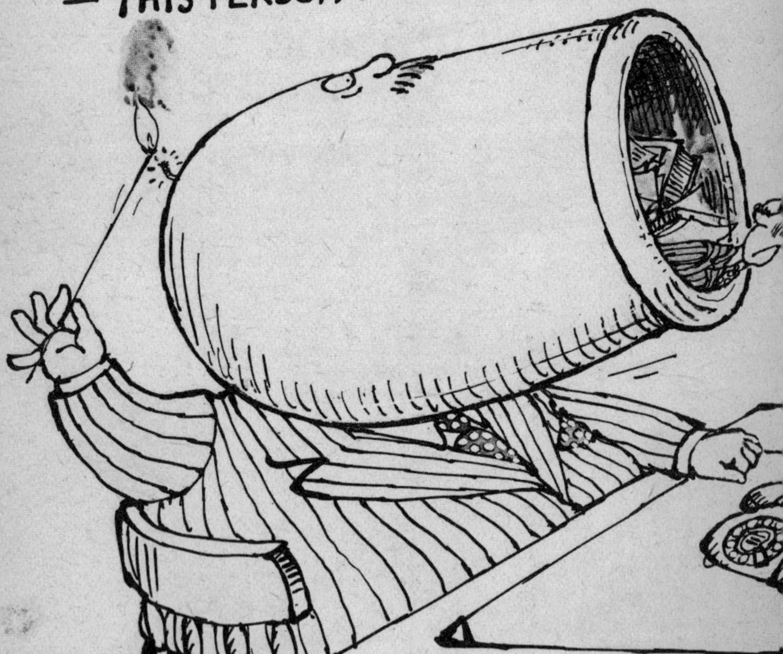

EXPLANATIONS OF CONSPICUOUS SUCCESS

The opulence of the office decor varies nversely with the fundamental solvency of the firm.

NDECISION IS THE BASIS FOR FLEXIBILITY.

HOW TO KILL AN ENTERPRISE.

1. Do not go to meetings.
2. If you go, arrive late.
3. Criticize the work of the organizers and members.
4. Get angry if you are not a member of the committee, but if you are, make no suggestions.

5. If the chair asks your opinion on a subject, say you have none. After the meeting say you learned nothing, or tell everyone what should have happened.
6. Don't do what has to be done yourself, but when the members roll up their sleeves and do their very best, complain that the group is run by a lot of ego-maniacs.
7. Complain that nothing is ever published which interests you but never offer to write an article, make a suggestion, or find a writer.
8. And if the enterprise dies, say you saw it coming ages ago!

Committee Life!

KILROY'S DEFINITION—

A committee meeting is an event at which the minutes are kept and the hours are lost.

THE LAW OF SUB-COMMITTE[E] FORMATION—

If you leave the room, you're elected.

THE RULE ON DECISION MAKING-
Never make a decision you can get someone else to make.

THE LAW OF LATE COMERS-
Those who have the shortest distance to a meeting invariably arrive the latest.

NO ONE KEEPS A RECORD OF YOUR GOOD DECISIONS: BUT EVERYONE KEEPS A RECORD OF YOUR BAD ONES!

Dealing with the Enemy

To make an enemy, do someone a favour.

DON'T LET YOUR SUPERIORS KNOW YOU'RE BETTER THAN THEY ARE.

when in trouble -

THE KENNEDY CONSTANT—
Don't get mad — get even!

NEVER ARGUE WITH A FOOL
—PEOPLE MIGHT NOT KNOW
THE DIFFERENCE!

Never attribute
to malice that which
is adequately explained
by stupidity.

WHEN YOUR OPPONENT
IS DOWN, KICK HIM!

People will believe anything
if you whisper it.

THE GADARENE SWINE LAW:

Merely because the group is in formation does not mean that the group is on the right course.

FRIENDS COME AND GO BUT ENEMIES ACCUMULATE.

Never offend people with style when you can offend them with substance.

Everything is possible.

EVERYTHING
IS POSSIBLE IF YOU DON'T
KNOW WHAT YOU'RE
TALKING ABOUT.

You can lead a horse to water, but if you can get him to float on his back, you've got something.

Financial Matters.

THE IRON LAW OF DISTRIBUTIO

Them that has, gets!

THE GOLDEN RULES OF ARTS AND SCIENCES-

Whoever has the gold makes the rule.

THE LAW OF MONETARY EQUALIZATION

A fool and your money are soon partner.

GETTY'S REMINDER–

The meek shall inherit the earth, but not its mineral rights.

TODD'S FIRST TWO POLITICAL PRINCIPLES

1 – No matter what they're telling you, they're not telling you the whole truth.

2 – No matter what they're talking about, they're talking about money.

CANADA BILL JONES MOTTO

IT'S MORALLY WRONG TO ALLOW SUCKERS TO KEEP THEIR MONEY.

SUPPLEMENT: A SMITH & WESSON BEATS FOUR ACES!

IN MATTERS OF DISPUTE, THE BANK'S BALANCE IS ALWAYS SMALLER THAN YOURS.

Live within your income even if you have to borrow to do so.

WHEN TWO PEOPLE MEET TO DECIDE HOW TO SPEND A THIRD PERSON'S MONEY, FRAUD WILL RESULT.

Expenditures rise to meet income.

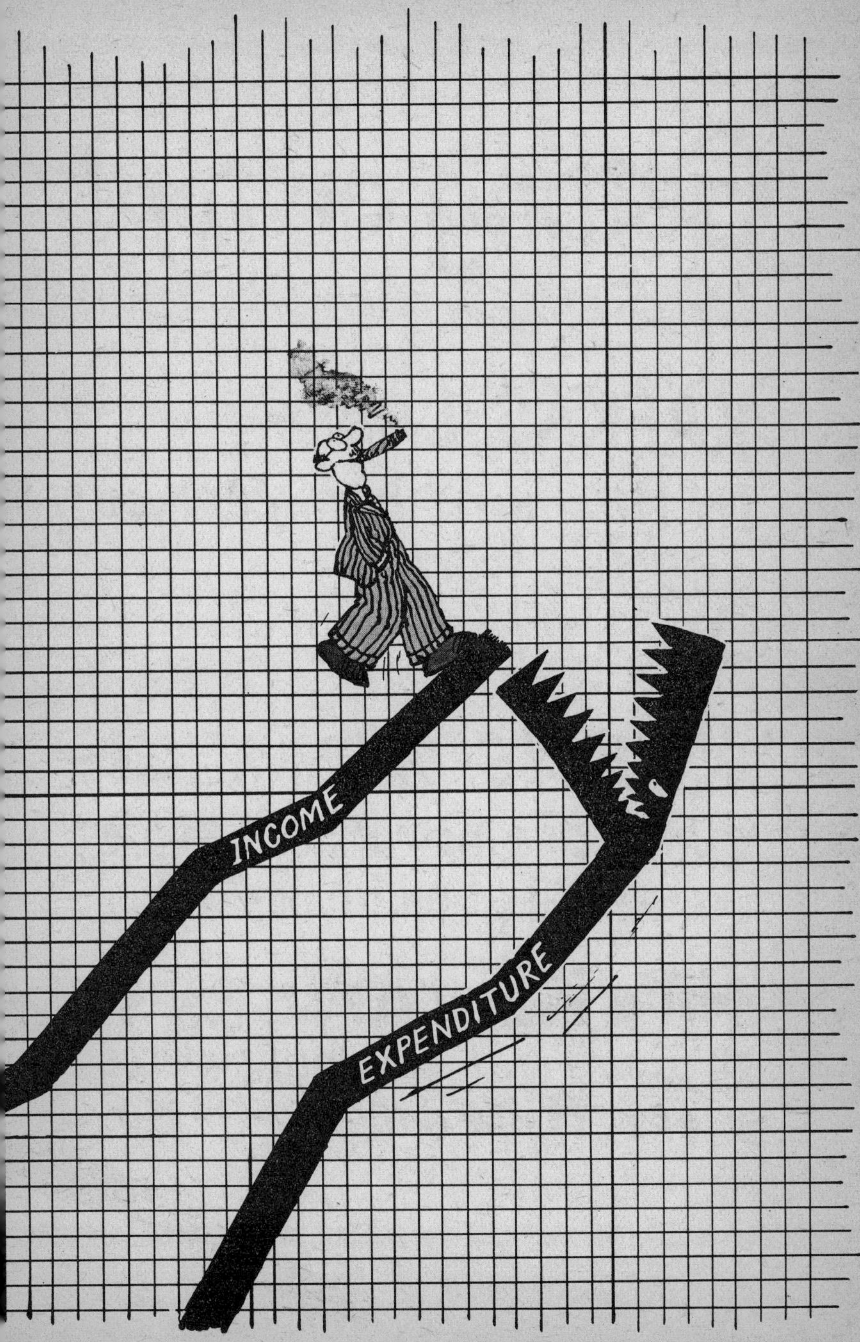
INCOME
EXPENDITURE

Getting on top!

KAFKA'S LAW—
In the fight between you
and the world,
— back the world.

KILROY'S OBSERVATION—
There are no winners in life;
— only survivors.

HAWK'S LAW—
If you find you can't suck seed
— try, try a wren.

THE LAW OF THE JUNGLE–

The lion and the lamb shall lie down together— but the lamb won't get much sleep.

COOK'S LAW

Creativity varies inversely with the number of cooks involved with the broth.

PETER'S PLACEBO

AN OUNCE OF IMAGE IS WORTH A POUND OF PERFORMANCE.

JAY'S FIRST LAW OF LEADERSHIP

CHANGING THINGS IS CENTRAL TO LEADERSHIP, AND CHANGING THEM BEFORE ANYONE ELSE IS CREATIVENESS.

SAGE'S LAW

You can make it foolproof, but you can't make it damnfoolproof.

How to be happy.

1- Accept that anything good in life is either illegal, immoral or fattening.

2- Realise that the three faithful things in life are money, a dog and an old woman.

3- Don't care if you're rich or not, as long as you can live comfortably and have everything you want.

General Rules -

1. ALWAYS DRIVE THROUGH AN AMBER LIGHT.
2. NEVER SAY NO.
3. THE YOUNGER, THE BETTER.

P.S. Never admit anything.
Never regret anything.
Whatever it is,
you're not responsible.

Never eat at a place called Mom's.
Never play cards with a man called Doc.
And never lie down with a woman who's got more troubles than you.

YOU CAN'T EXPECT TO HIT THE JACKPOT IF YOU DON'T PUT A FEW NICKELS IN THE MACHINE.

Instant Relaxation.

LAW OF LEISURE—

If, in the course of several months, only three worthwhile social events take place, they will all fall on the same evening.

RULE OF FELINE FRUSTRATION·

When your cat has fallen asleep on your lap and looks utterly content and adorable you will suddenly have to go to the lavatory.

LAW OF THE FRONT ROW–
Fools rush in – and get the best seats.

LAW OF REPEATS–
If you have watched a TV series only once, and you watch it again, it will be a repeat of the same episode.

LAW OF SPECTATOR SPORTS–
Exciting play occurs and goals are scored only while you are out of the room!

Laws of Gardening

1. Other people's tools work only in other people's gardens.
2. Fancy gadgets don't work.

3. If nobody uses it, there must be a reason.

4. You get the most of what you need least.

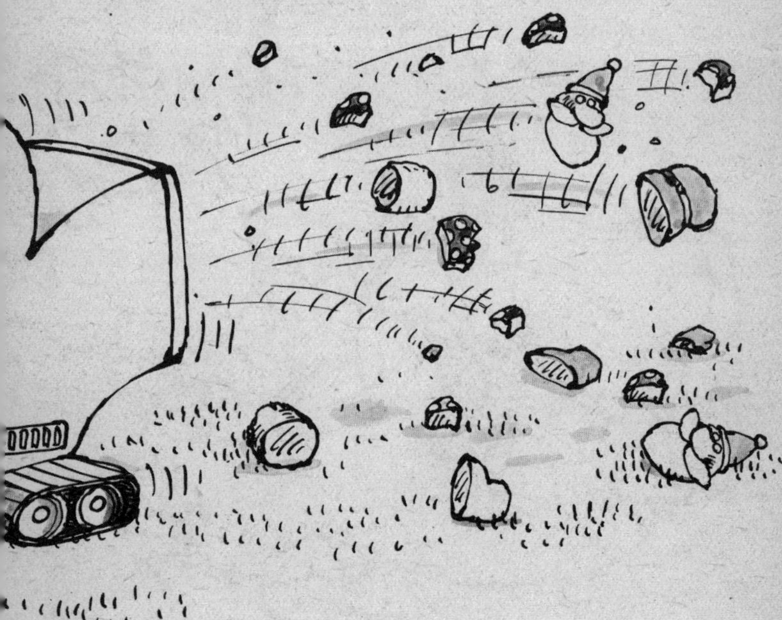

Juvenile Law.

THE INEVITABLES OF PARENTHOOD

1. Enough is never enough.
2. Birthday parties always end in tears (usually five minutes before you decide to take the children home.)

. Any child who chatters non-stop at home will adamantly refuse to utter a word when requested to demonstrate for an audience.

1. Any shy, introverted child will choose a crowded public area to loudly demonstrate newly acquired vocabulary (damn, penis, sod, bugger, etc., etc.)

THE LAW OF CLEANLINESS

A child will not spill anything on a dirty floor.

THE LAW OF DESTRUCTION

A unbreakable toy is useful for breaking other toys.

THE LAW OF CONSTRUCTION

Give a small boy a hammer and he will find that everything he encounters needs pounding.

CHRISTMAS MORNING, THE FIRST DISCOVERY OF:
Batteries not included!

THE LAWS OF ADOLESCENCE

You can fool all of the people some of the time and some of the people all of the time, but you can't fool MUM!

The scratch on the record is through the long track you like most.

THE PIMPLES DON'T APPEAR UNTIL THE HOUR BEFORE THE HOUR!

Kitchen Lore.

1. Soufflés rise and cream whips only for the family and for guests who you didn't really want to invite.
2. The rotten egg will be the one you break into the cake batter.

3. Any cooking utensil placed in the dishwater will be needed immediately thereafter for something else; any measuring utensil used for liquid ingredients will be needed immediately thereafter for dry ingredients.

4. Time spent consuming a meal is in inverse proportion to time spent preparing it.

5. Whatever it is, somebody will have had it for lunch!

THE CITRUS OBSERVATION

THERE ARE THIRTY-TWO POINTS TO THE COMPASS, MEANING THAT THERE ARE THIRTY-TWO DIRECTIONS IN WHICH A SPOON CAN SQUIRT GRAPEFRUIT, YET THE JUICE ALMOST INVARIABLY FLIES STRAIGHT INTO THE HUMAN EYE!

HE LAW OF KITCHEN SURFACES

:leanliness is next to impossible!

THE PERFECT PHILOSOPHY

Everybody should
elieve in something;
—I believe I'll have another drink.

Looking good.

THE LAW OF APPEARANCE

Beauty is only skin deep, but ugly goes clean to the bone.

COBBLER'S LAW

If the shoe fits — it's ugly!

THE LAW OF FASHION

THE SAME DRESS IS:

- ☆ INDECENT TEN YEARS BEFORE ITS TIME.
- ☆ DARING ONE YEAR BEFORE ITS TIME.
- ☆ CHIC IN ITS TIME.
- ☆ DOWDY THREE YEARS AFTER ITS TIME.
- ☆ HIDEOUS TWENTY YEARS AFTER ITS TIME.
- ☆ AMUSING THIRTY YEARS AFTER ITS TIME.
- ☆ ROMANTIC A HUNDRED YEARS AFTER ITS TIME.
- ☆ BEAUTIFUL A HUNDRED AND FIFTY YEARS AFTER ITS TIME.

Marriage Lines

THE LAW OF MARITAL BLISS
Most people deserve each other!

'HE MATRIMONIAL EQUATION

'he length of a marriage is inversely ·roportional to the amount spent n the wedding.

'HE GREEN CROSS MOTHER-IN-LAW CODE

;top - Look - Listen - Run!

THE LAW OF INFIDELITY

THE PROBABILITY OF MEETING SOMEONE YOU KNOW INCREASES WHEN YOU ARE WITH SOMEONE YOU DON'T WANT TO BE SEEN WITH.

BEDFELLOW'S RULE–

The one who snores will fall asleep first.

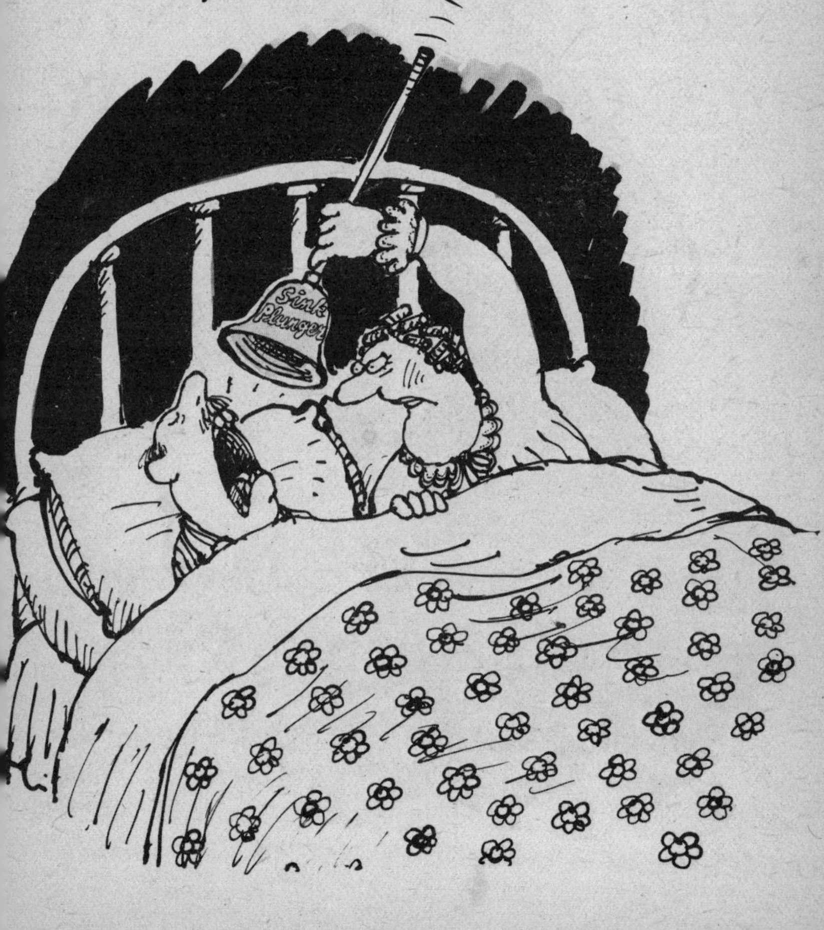

Nuts and Bolts.

When all else fails read the instruction

IT WORKS BETTER IF YOU PLUG IT IN

If at first you don't succeed – cry, cry agai

TROUBLE STRIKES IN SERIES OF THREES, BUT WHEN WORKING AROUND THE HOUSE, THE NEXT CATASTROPHE AFTER A SERIES OF THREE IS NOT THE FOURTH ONE —IT'S A START OF A BRAND NEW SERIES OF THREE!

If it jams – force it. If it breaks, it needs replacing

It's better to have a horrible ending than to have horrors without end.

Optimism.

THE MAN WHO CAN SMILE WHEN THINGS GO WRONG HAS THOUGHT OF SOMEONE HE CAN BLAME IT ON.

It does not matter if you fall down as long as you pick up something from the floor while you get up

THERE IS NO TIME LIKE THE PRESENT FOR POSTPONING WHAT YOU DON'T WANT TO DO.

RULE FOR DETERMINING OLD AGE.

Old age is always 15 years older than I am.

Pessimism.

AN OPTIMIST BELIEVES WE LIVE IN THE BEST OF ALL POSSIBLE WORLDS —A PESSIMIST FEARS THIS IS TRUE.

You can't tell how deep a puddle is until you step in it.

OPPORTUNITY ALWAYS KNOCKS AT THE LEAST OPPORTUNE MOMENT.

Nothing is ever so bad that it can't get worse.

BLESSED IS HE WHO EXPECTS NOTHING, FOR HE SHALL NOT BE DISAPPOINTED.

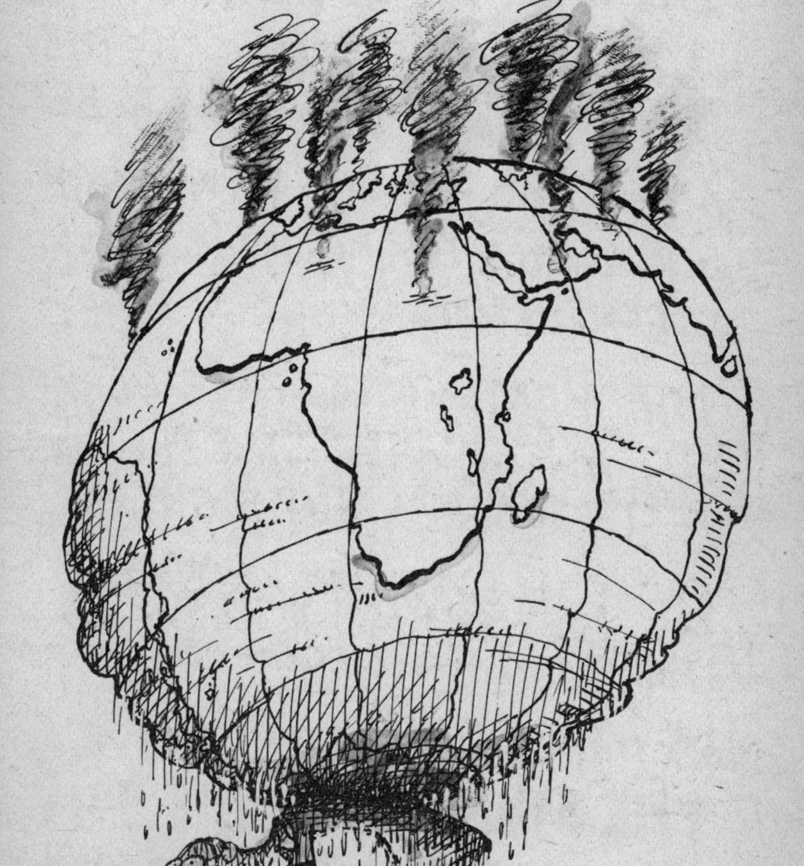

THE RACE IS NOT ALWAYS TO THE SWIFT, NOR THE BATTLE TO THE STRONG, BUT THAT'S THE WAY TO BET.

After things have gone from bad to worse, the cycle will repeat itself.

THE MOMENT YOU HAVE WORKED OUT AN ANSWER, START CHECKING IT — IT PROBABLY ISN'T RIGHT.

No matter what goes wrong, there is always somebody who knew it would.

THE MURPHY PHILOSOPHY

SMILE — TOMORROW WILL BE WORSE!

Every time you come up with a terrific idea, you find someone else thought of it first.

NO GOOD DEED
GOES UNPUNISHED.

When you need
to knock on wood is
when you realise the
world's composed of
aluminium and vinyl.
TING!

EVAN'S LAW

If you can keep your head when all about you are losing theirs, then you just don't understand the problem.

ELIOT'S OBSERVATION

Nothing is so good as it seems beforehand.

IF YOU FEEL GOOD, DON'T WORRY.
—YOU'LL SOON GET OVER IT!

THE WORKER'S DILEMMA

1- No matter how much you do, you'll never do enough.
2- What you <u>don't</u> do is always more important than what you <u>do</u> do.

GIVE UP DURING LENT!!

It is impossible for an optimist to be pleasantly surprised.

MISERY NO LONGER LOVES COMPANY..... NOWADAYS IT INSISTS ON IT.

Queue here.

THE BARGAIN RULE

No matter how long or how hard you shop for an item, after you've bought it it'll be on sale somewhere cheaper.

THE CONSUMER'S DILEMMA–

If it's good..... they discontinue it.

THE PRICE LAW

If an item is advertised 'as under £50', you can bet it's not £19-50.

NEVER DECIDE TO BUY SOMETHING WHILE LISTENING TO THE SALESMAN.

THE SALES LAW

The one you want is never the one on sale.

HADLEY'S LAW OF SHOPPING FOR CLOTHES

1- If you like it, they don't have it in your size.
2- If you like it and it's in your size, it doesn't fit anyway.
3- If you like it and it fits, you can't afford it.
4- If you like it, it fits and you can afford it, it falls apart the first time you wear it.

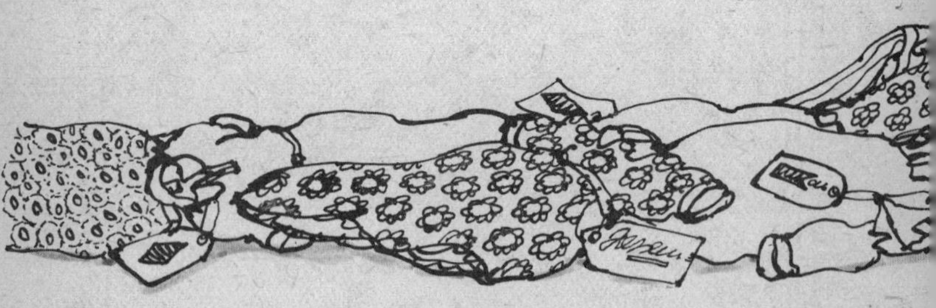

Restaurant Fare

THE CANTEEN LAW

The item you had your eye on the minute you walked in will be taken by the person in front of you.

INSTITUTIONAL FOOD, LAWS OF

1- Everything is cold except what should be.

2- Everything, including the cornflakes, is greasy.

NO MAN IS LONELY WHILE EATING SPAGHETTI

THE RULE OF THE GREAT

When somebody you greatly and respect appears to be thinking deep thoughts, they probably thinking about LUNCH!

THE FREE LUNCH RULE

There's no such thing as a free lunc

COLE'S LAW—

THINLY SLICED CABBAG

THE GOURMET'S LAW

EVERYTHING TASTES MORE OR LESS
LIKE CHICKEN.

DEAN MARTIN'S DEFINITION OF DRUNKENNESS

You're not drunk if you can lie on the floor without holding on.

THE THREE RULES FOR TRYING NEW FOODS

1 - Never try anything with tomatoes in it.

2 - Never try anything bigger than your head.

3 - Never, never try anything that looks like vomit

Break all the rules
— and have a PIZZA!!

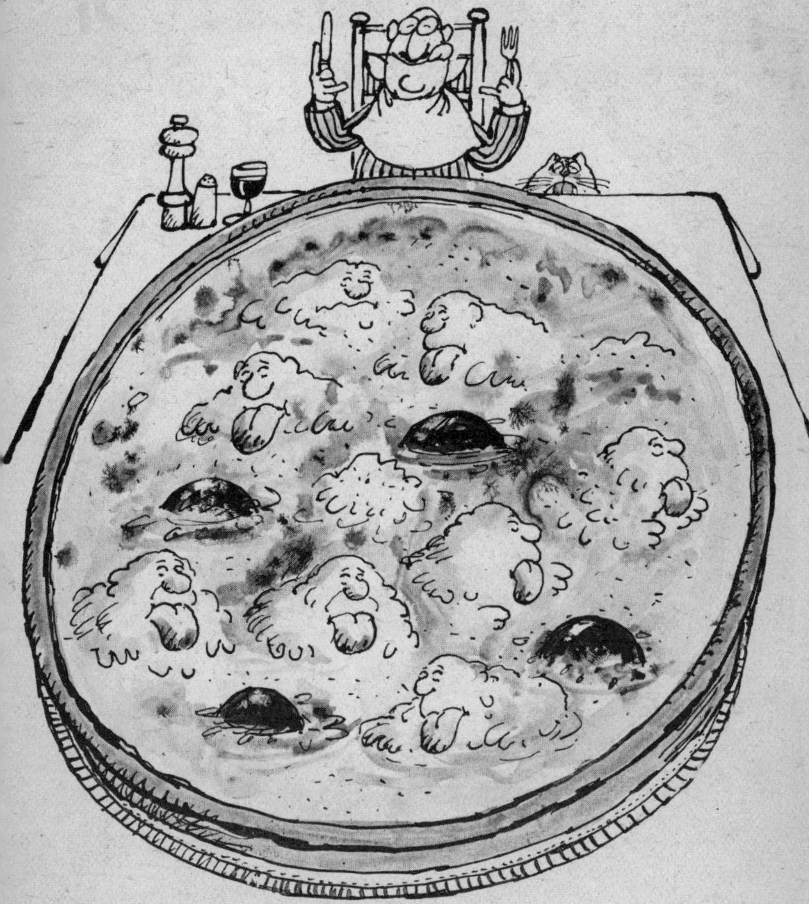

INSTANT GUIDE TO MODERN SCIENCE
1- If it's green or it wriggles, it's biology.
2-If it stinks, it's chemistry.
3-If it doesn't work, it's physics
GROUND RULE FOR LABORATORY WORKERS
When you don't know what you are doing, do it neatly.
If A equals success, then the formula A=X+Y+Z. X=work. Y=play. Z=keep your mouth shut.

THE FIRST RULE OF SCIENTIFIC RESEARCH

Do not believe in miracles
— Rely on them!

YOUNG'S LAW

All great discoveries are made by mistake.

COROLLARY: The greater the funding, the longer it takes to make the mistake.

THE COMPLETE LAWS OF UNRELIABILITY

1- Computers are unreliable, but humans are even more unreliable.

2- Any system which depends on human reliability is unreliable.

3- Undetectable errors are infinite in variety, in contrast to detectable errors, which by definition are limited.

4- Investments in reliabity will increase until it exceeds the probable cost of errors, or until someone insists on getting some useful work done.

A COMPUTER PROGRAMME DOES WHAT YOU TELL IT TO DO, NOT WHAT YOU WANT IT TO DO.

To err is human, but to really foul things up requires a computer.

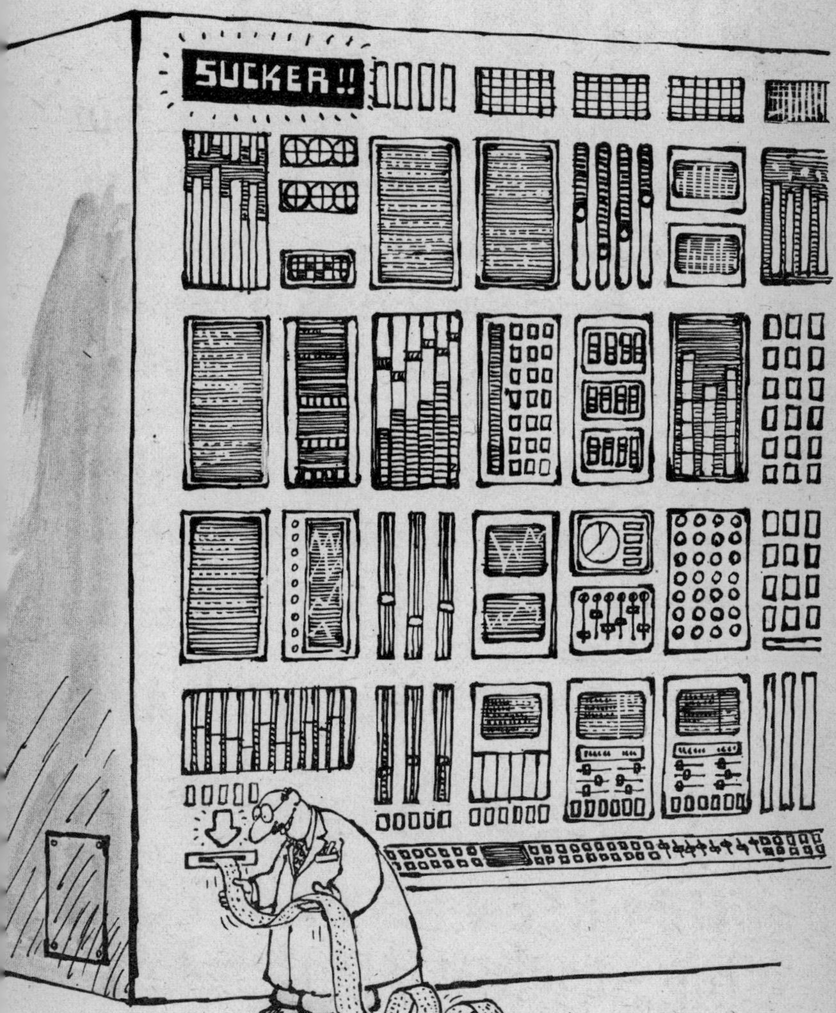
SUCKER!!

Travel light.

THE FIRST LAW OF BICYCLING

No matter which way you ride, it's uphill and against the wind.

THE LAW OF LIFE'S HIGHWAY

If everything is coming your way, you're in the wrong lane.

THE FIRST LAW OF TRAVEL

It always takes longer to get there than to get back

THE GREEN HEDGEHOG CODE

Stop – Look – Listen ... but not in the middle of the road.

THE AUTOMOTIVE LAWS

1 - Nothing minor ever happens to a car at the weekend.

2 - Nothing minor ever happens to a car on a trip.

3 - Nothing minor ever happens to a car.

CORCORONI'S LAW OF BUS TRANSPORTATION

1- The bus that left the stop just before you got there was your bus.

2- The amount of time you have to wait for a bus is directly proportional to the inclemency of the weather.

3- All buses heading in the opposite direction drive off the face of the earth and never return.

4- The last rush-hour express bus to your district leaves five minutes before you get off work.

5- Bus schedules are arranged so that your bus will arrive at the transfer point precisely one minute after the connecting bus has gone.

6- Any bus that can be the wrong bus will be the wrong bus:
— All others are out of service or full.

VOYAGER II
11
KATTO

THE EXCHANGE RATE AXIOM

When travelling overseas, the exchange rate improves markedly the day after one has purchased foreign currency.

COROLLARY:
Upon returning home, the rate drops again as soon as one has converted all unused foreign currency.

THE IN-FLIGHT LAW

As soon as the steward serves the coffee, the airliner always encounters turbulence.

THE LAW OF LOCATION

NO MATTER WHERE YOU GO, THERE YOU ARE!

LONGFELLOW'S RULES FOR LIFTS

1 - FACE FORWARD.
2 - FOLD HANDS IN FRONT.
3 - DO NOT MAKE EYE CONTACT.
4 - WATCH THE NUMBERS.
5 - DON'T TALK TO ANYONE YOU DON'T KNOW.
6 - STOP TALKING WITH ANYONE YOU DO KNOW WHEN ANYONE YOU DON'T KNOW ENTERS THE LIFT.
7 - AVOID BRUSHING BODIES.

THE LAW OF LIFT POSITIONING

Passengers in lifts constantly rearrange their positions as people get on and off so there is at all times an equal distance between all bodies.

Under doctor's orders.

THE FIRST LAW OF MEDICIN

pills taken in twos always com
out of the bottle in threes.

THE DENTAL LAW

Toothache tends to start on Saturday night.

THE LAW OF LOCAL ANAESTHESIA

Never say 'oops' in the operating theatre.

THE DEFINITION OF ALCOHOLISM

An alcoholic is a person who drinks more than his or her own physician.

SIX PRINCIPLES FOR PATIENT

1- JUST BECAUSE YOUR DOCTOR HAS A NAME FOR YOUR CONDITION DOESN'T MEAN HE KNOWS WHAT IT IS

2- ONLY ADULTS HAVE DIFFICULTY WITH CHILD-PROOF BOTTLES.

3- THE MORE BORING OR OUT-OF-DAT THE MAGAZINES ARE IN THE WAITIN ROOM, THE LONGER YOU'LL HAVE TO WAIT FOR YOUR SCHEDULED APPOINTMENT.

4 - YOU NEVER HAVE THE RIGHT NUMBER OF PILLS LEFT ON THE LAST DAY OF A PRESCRIPTION.

5.- THE PILLS TO BE TAKEN WITH MEALS WILL BE THE LEAST APPETIZING ONES. (EVEN WATER TASTES BAD WHEN TAKEN ON DOCTOR'S ORDERS).

6 - IF YOUR CONDITION SEEMS TO BE GETTING BETTER, IT'S PROBABLY YOUR DOCTOR GETTING SICK.

Vice is nice!

ARTHUR'S LAWS OF LOVE

1- THE LOVE LETTER YOU FINALLY GOT THE COURAGE TO SEND WILL BE DELAYED IN THE POST LONG ENOUGH FOR YOU TO MAKE A FOOL OF YOURSELF IN PERSON.

2- PEOPLE WHOM YOU ARE ATTRACTED TO, INVARIABLY THINK YOU REMIND THEM OF SOMEONE ELSE.

3- OTHER PEOPLE'S ROMANTIC GESTURES SEEM NOVEL AND EXCITING. YOUR OWN ROMANTIC GESTURES SEEM FOOLISH AND CLUMSY.

4- NEVER GET EXCITED ABOUT A BLIND DATE BECAUSE OF HOW IT SOUNDS ON THE 'PHONE.

5- NEVER GET EXCITED ABOUT A PERSON BECAUSE OF WHAT THEY LOOK LIKE FROM BEHIND.

THE FARMER'S CREDO-

Sow your wild oats on Saturday night – then on Sunday pray for crop failure.

THE SANITY RULE

Never sleep with anyone who's crazier than yourself.

THE FAMILY WAY

Sex is hereditary – If your parents never had it, the chances are you won't either.

FIRST LAW OF SOCIO-GENETICS-

CELIBACY IS NOT HEREDITARY

The probability of a young man meeting a desirable receptive young female increases by pyramidal progression when he is already in the company of:-

1 — a date.
2 — his wife.
3 — a better looking and richer male friend.

NO MATTER HOW MANY TIMES YOU'VE HAD IT, IF IT'S OFFERED, TAKE IT, BECAUSE IT'LL NEVER BE QUITE THE SAME AGAIN.

Words of Wisdom.

LAWS OF TRUTH IN REPORTING

1 - The closer you are to the facts of a situation, the more obvious are the errors in all news coverage of the situation.

2 - The further you are from the facts of a situation, the more you tend to believe news coverage of the situation.

THE GREEN CROSS SCOOP CODE

STOP - LOOK - LISTEN - FABRICATE !!

LAW OF EDITORIAL CORRECTION

Anyone nit-picking enough to write a letter of correction to an editor deserves the error that has provoked it

THE FIRST LAW OF JOURNALISM

The further away the disaster or accident occurs, the greater number of dead and injured required for it to become a story.

A MAN WITH ONE WATCH
KNOWS WHAT TIME IT IS.
A MAN WITH TWO WATCHES
IS NEVER SURE.

Blessed are the pure in heart
—eventually.

Any task worth doing was
worth doing yesterday.

A PIPE GIVES A WISE MAN
TIME TO THINK AND A FOOL
SOMETHING TO STICK IN HIS MOUTH.

Necessity is the mother of strange bedfellows.

BUILD A SYSTEM THAT EVEN A FOOL CAN USE, AND ONLY A FOOL WILL WANT TO USE IT

If you don't care where you are, you ain't lost!

There are four kinds of people: Those who sit quietly and do nothing: Those who talk about sitting quietly and doing nothing: Those who do things; And those who talk about doing things.

KILROY'S CORRECTION:

THERE ARE TWO TYPES OF PEOPLE: THOSE WHO DIVIDE PEOPLE INTO TYPES AND THOSE WHO DON'T.

Xpert advice.

EXPERT ADVICE, THE FIRST LAW OF:

Don't ask the barber whether you need a haircut.

THE EXPERT DEFINITION

An expert is one who knows more and more about less and less until he knows absolutely everything about nothing.

FINDING THE EXPERT

To spot the expert, pick the one who predicts the job will take the longest and cost the most.

THE SAUSAGE PRINCIPLE

PEOPLE WHO LOVE SAUSAGE AND RESPECT THE LAW SHOULD NEVER WATCH EITHER ONE BEING MADE.

You'd better face up to it!

Nobody really cares or understands what anyone else is doing

WASHING YOUR CAR TO MAKE IT RAIN DOESN'T WORK.

If a situation requires undivided attention, it will occur simultaneously with a compelling distraction.

WHEN THE LAW IS AGAINST YOU, ARGUE THE FACTS. WHEN THE FACTS ARE AGAINST YOU, ARGUE THE LAW. WHEN BOTH ARE AGAINST YOU, CALL THE OTHER LAWYER NAMES.

A CRISIS IS WHEN YOU CAN'T SAY 'LET'S FORGET THE WHOLE THING.'

THE LAW OF PROBABLE DISPERSAL

Whatever hits the fan will not be evenly distributed.

WELLINGTON'S LAW OF COMMAND

THE CREAM RISES TO THE TOP
— SO DOES THE SCUM !!

THE LAW OF FRIENDSHIP

If you help a friend in need, he is sure to remember you — the next time he's in need!

THE FEMALE EQUATION

Whatever women do, they must do twice as well as men to be thought half as good:
— Luckily, this is not difficult!

Zhat's life!

THE SMOKE LAW

The tendency of cigarette smok
to drift into a person's face varie
directly with that person's sensitivity
to smoke.

THE LAW EXPLAINING WHY THAT'S ZHAT

IF YOU HIT TWO KEYS ON THE TYPEWRITER, THE ONE YOU DON'T WANT HITS THE PAPER!

If you're early, it'll be cancelled.
If you kill yourself to be on time you will have to wait.
If you're late, you will be too late

THE LIFE EXPECTANCY OF A HOUSE PLANT, VARIES INVERSELY WITH ITS PRICE AND DIRECTLY WITH ITS UGLINESS.

You can always find what you're not looking for.

EINSTEIN'S OTHER LAW OF RELATIVITY

How long a minute is, depends on which side of the lavatory door you're on.

IF YOU MISS ONE ISSUE OF ANY MAGAZINE IT WILL BE THE ISSUE WHICH CONTAINED THE ARTICLE, STORY OR INSTALMENT YOU WERE MOST ANXIOUS TO READ. —WHAT'S MORE, ALL YOUR FRIENDS EITHER MISSED IT, LOST IT OR THREW IT AWAY YESTERDAY.

Bare feet magnetise sharp metal objects so they always point upwards from the floor — especially in the dark!

THE BEST WAY TO INSPIRE FRESH THOUGHTS IS TO SEAL THE LETTER.

No books are lost by lending except those you particularly wanted to keep.

ALEXANDER GRAHAM BELL'S TELEPHONE LAW

1 - The telephone will ring when you are outside the door, fumbling for your keys
2 - You will reach it just in time to hear the click of the caller hanging up.
3 - When you dial a wrong number, you never get an engaged signal.

THE UMBRELLA LAW

YOU WILL NEED 3 UMBRELLAS;

- ONE TO LEAVE AT THE OFFICE.
- ONE TO LEAVE AT HOME.
- ONE TO LEAVE ON THE TRAIN.

THE CLAWS CLAUSE

Whenever you cut your nails you will find a need for them later.

1ST

Kilroy's Law

HE WHO LAUGHS LAST
— PROBABLY DIDN'T
GET THE JOKE!